~~Teddy's Tail~~
Teddy Tales

TRUE STORIES OF A SCHOOL THERAPY DOG

Karla (Wunderlin) Unke

authorHOUSE®

AuthorHouse™
1663 Liberty Drive
Bloomington, IN 47403
www.authorhouse.com
Phone: 1 (800) 839-8640

Published by AuthorHouse 10/16/2015

ISBN: 978-1-5049-4804-3 (sc)
ISBN: 978-1-5049-4803-6 (e)

Library of Congress Control Number: 2015914450

Print information available on the last page.

Any people depicted in stock imagery provided by Thinkstock are models, and such images are being used for illustrative purposes only.
Certain stock imagery © Thinkstock.

This book is printed on acid-free paper.

CONTENTS

Contents Continued

Bonus Section
(pages 54-82)

DEDICATION

I dedicate this book to my children, Shawn, Brian, and Claire, who shared their beloved dog (and their mom) with hundreds of other children at school over the years. You three never once minded stopping for Teddy's "fan club" when we were out, or to hear another story about him from someone. Jealousy never once entered your hearts, only love and kindness.

To my step children, Austin and Kylee, thank you for always showing love and kindness to this fabulous family dog of ours. Though you've never seen him "in action" at school, you've always known just how special a dog he is!

From the Author

As the school counselor, I was blessed to be the handler of Teddy, our school's first, and our district's third therapy dog. He came to me as a one year old puppy in need of a home.

Our PTA had approved paying for a therapy dog from CARES, Inc in Concordia, Kansas. I was on the waiting list for a Golden Retriever therapy dog for our school. In December of 2002, I learned a middle school teacher had moved to an apartment and could no longer care for his one year old Golden Retriever named "Teddy." My principal called CARES, Inc. and asked them if we could bring our own dog out to be trained instead of getting one of theirs. They said this would work. We adopted Teddy right away and had him trained in March of 2003. Just like that, I entered into one of the most rewarding experiences of my career!

Over the years, I have seen countless ways this dog has helped both students and adults. Teddy was known by over 2,500 students in his 12+

years as a Certified Professional Therapy Dog. His impact has been tremendous. I relay only a portion of the stories to you here. Some stories were as simple as, "My son said he was feeling sad at school and Teddy just walked by and he said he felt better!" Even at home, when my children are hurt or crying, he instinctively goes to them. Therapy dogs in schools are an amazing benefit to all students. They can transform lives. Currently, three of our four elementary schools, and our middle school have a therapy dog. I'm very thankful my school district in Clinton, Iowa has been supportive of them for our students!

I hope you enjoy this collection of true stories and remember Teddy's motto: There's always time to "paws" for a little TLC (Teddy's Loving Care)!

Karla (Wunderlin) Unke

*The names of individuals have been changed in some stories to respect their privacy.

CHAPTER 1

A Sad Spring for Tyler

Teddy instinctively knew when a student (or anyone, for that matter) needed him to be calmed. They say we humans give off a scent when we are upset which dogs can smell and some will react to, such as Teddy.

It was spring and Easter was fast approaching. I had been working with a young man in third grade whose father had passed away. It was close to a year since his passing, and the boy was struggling with the anniversary date of his dad's death approaching. While I worked with Tyler, Teddy would lie at Tyler's feet. During moments of extreme sadness, Tyler would begin to cry. When this would happen, Teddy would stand up and gently lay his head on Tyler's lap. As Tyler would pet Teddy's head, he would begin to calm and regain control of his emotions.

On the actual anniversary date of his dad's death, Tyler came to see me in the morning. He was shaken, but prepared himself for the day ahead of him. His mom had called earlier and told me she would like Tyler to stay at school if at all possible that day. I told Tyler if he had trouble getting through his day, to come see me. I let his teacher know I would make myself available if he needed help.

As lunch time approached, I stepped out of my office briefly and Teddy remained lying in his usual spot, just inside the thresh hold of my doorway. Evidently, Tyler began to have trouble, and came to see me, crying. Our principal was in his office, which was right across the hall from mine. He heard Tyler crying and came over to see what was wrong. He recounted to me later, as Tyler cried and told him about the reason for his sadness, that Teddy instinctively went to Tyler and "buried his head in that boy's lap." The principal was shocked and amazed at not only this act, but also the effect of Teddy's presence as Tyler began to calm and go back to class.

Even later in the day, I sat at my desk working, Teddy in his usual place. He rarely left the thresh hold of my door. Suddenly, Teddy bound to his feet and left my doorway, heading down the hall, three doors away, to the Nurse's office. This wasn't like Teddy to leave my side, so I rose and followed him. What I saw was heartwarming.

Tyler had begun to have what appeared to be a panic attack, having trouble breathing and tightness in his chest, so his teacher sent him to see the nurse. Teddy sensed this, and immediately went to Tyler's side. He laid his head in Tyler's lap once again, his big brown eyes gazing up at Tyler. The nurse and I were amazed and in awe of the scene before us! Tyler began petting Teddy, calmed once again, and was able to go back to class and get through this very difficult day.

When Teddy saw me watching, he tucked his tail, as if he thought he were in trouble for leaving my office area. Of course, I only praised him for knowing what to do and doing it!

Teddy heard Tyler in the nurse's office and instinctively knew he needed emotional support more than medical help, so he rose and went to him. Tyler, receiving Teddy's loving care, calmed enough to feel better and go back to class. What an amazing scene!

CHAPTER 2

Not Just Scared ...
Terrified of Dogs

Many students have fears of dogs, for many different reasons. Some have had a previous bad experience with other dogs. Others, especially small children, are simply overwhelmed since the dog is as big as they are and they find themselves face to face with the hot breath of a dog's jowls! Whatever the reason, I've never seen a girl as frightened of a dog as Chelsey.

It was early in the school year and a new student had moved into Whittier, Chelsey. Many students, especially kindergarteners, would come in somewhat hesitant of dogs to start with, but once they saw Teddy's calm manner, they would easily lay their fears aside, at least when it came to Teddy! Teddy had been at Whittier for many years, and all students were accustomed to seeing him in the hallways with me.

One particular afternoon, I was heading into a kindergarten classroom when I passed by Chelsey's first grade classroom leaving their room to go to Music. Chelsey saw Teddy and immediately went into a total and complete state of panic. She backed herself up against the lockers and screamed and cried and literally shook her hands with fear. Surprised by this, I turned to see her teacher on one knee at Chelsey's eye level and telling her in her calmest, sweetest voice, to calm down. This was not working. Chelsey continued and even escalated.

Her teacher said, "This is Teddy. He is our school dog. He's really calm. He won't hurt you."

But Chelsey was too terrified to hear anything. Her teacher held her face gently in her hands and told her to just simply look at her instead of Teddy. Chelsey reluctantly did this, giving quick, panic stricken side glances in his direction. I took Teddy into the classroom where we were headed, and let her go with Chelsey. The trauma was over for now but I knew we had a severe problem if this little girl was going to be at Whittier and see our therapy dog frequently.

I phoned her mom and described what I had witnessed with regard to Chelsey. Her mom said she had no idea where Chelsey had gotten such an intense fear of dogs, but knew she had one. She didn't want her to grow up afraid of dogs, and asked if somehow Teddy and I could get her daughter over this fear. I eagerly agreed and assured her we had never had anyone afraid of Teddy for very long. Once they saw how calm and loving he was, and witnessed their classmates affectionately interacting with him, they quickly came to know he would not harm them.

I began working with Chelsey alone without Teddy. Chelsey stated she didn't know why she had this fear of dogs, but also decided she would like to be past it. Her desire to be over the fear of dogs would definitely make the process easier. I told her Teddy and I would help.

I began the first day by asking Chelsey simply touch his tail. She once again panicked and literally shook her fists in fear, unable to even reach her hand toward Teddy. I knew this would be more involved than I imagined. I decided

I needed to back up even more and begin by letting her simply get used to seeing Teddy and build on that.

With her teacher's help, I prepared her for daily "pass-bys" of Teddy. This involved her simply standing in the hall and watching Teddy walk past her. Once again, this led to screams of utter terror, so we backed up and had her stand inside her classroom, look through the window and watch Teddy walk by. Thankfully, this worked. I did this daily, sometimes twice a day, for about a week.

Next, I had Chelsey stand back in the hall and watch Teddy go by. This also worked! After about another week of this, I had her touch his tail. With extreme caution, she did so. The look on her face was one I'll never forget. It was a combination of happiness, anxiety, and pride, as she touched his tail for a brief moment. After that, she petted his tail successfully. Teddy, sensing her fear, never once made any quick movements around her, nor did he approach her – he let her take the lead and approach him. In the weeks to come, she gradually increased her contact with Teddy until she was able to pet his head and even give him a treat!

It took Chelsey longer than any student in Teddy's 12.5 years at Whittier, but she did overcome her fear of dogs, at least of Teddy! I shared periodically with her mother, how it was going. Her mother was extremely grateful for the help and used the methods to help Chelsey eventually overcome her fear of other dogs! By Halloween, Chelsey had overcome her fear entirely!

Teddy's calm mannerism helped Chelsey realize she had nothing to fear in him. She gradually got used to seeing Teddy increasing her contact with him. Teddy, sensing her fear, kept his distance until she was ready to pet him. I'll never forget later that Spring, when Chelsey willingly stopped Teddy in the commons and lay her face alongside his. She gently caressed his ears and spoke lovingly to him. Realizing how far she had come, both her teacher and I watched with a combination of awe and happiness at this scene before us. I let my heart take a picture!

The Nursing Home Visit

Teddy made occasional visits to the nursing home if we knew someone was there who might enjoy seeing him. He visited my own grandmother back in my hometown of Platteville, Wisconsin while she was in the nursing home. My grandmother was a lifetime dog lover and both she and Teddy soaked up the love while he visited her!

We were on one such visit on a Sunday afternoon, leaving a skilled care nursing home in Clinton. Teddy "heeled" very well and never was one to pull on the leash. This time, as we passed a room, he pulled on the leash, beckoning me to follow him into what seemed to be a random room. Not knowing who was in there, I was hesitant, until I noticed a coworker of mine, Julie, at the bedside of a woman lying asleep. Julie looked drained, but an immediate smile sprang to her face as she saw Teddy. She invited us in. Teddy loved Julie, as she was a teacher who kept treats in her room at school! Whenever Teddy would visit her room, she had a treat for him. We laughed together as we made note that Teddy must have been expecting her to have a treat ready and waiting; however, oddly, he seemed only mildly interested in Julie this day. Instead, he was curious about the individual lying in the hospital bed.

She told us this was her cousin who had been quite ill for a long time and introduced us. Her cousin was so weak she could barely get out a thin sounding "hello," but raised her eyes to Teddy. Julie told me her cousin was a lifetime dog lover and asked if Teddy would put his front paws up on the bed so she could see him. As I gave Teddy the command, he softly raised just his front paws to the bed. He was incredibly calm as he ever so gently balanced himself and greeted her cousin.

He seemed to hold such a calm restraint over himself, as if he realized just how sick this woman was. Her cousin weakly raised her hand to stroke Teddy's soft head and ears with one hand. It seemed to be all she could do to lift her arm, heavy with IV's. A slow grin grew on her lips as she stroked his soft head.

"He's soft," she whispered, and she dropped her hand back to her side. "Thank you," she said, and closed her eyes again.

Julie thanked me for taking a moment to see her, and we left.

Later I learned that just a couple of days before Teddy's visit, Julie's cousin had been told there was nothing more the doctors could do for her. She said her daughters and other family members had tried to keep talking with her about happy memories to keep her spirits up. Julie explained after Teddy left, her cousin began talking about her own dogs she had had over the years, and her happy memories of them.

A few days later, back at school, Teddy and I stopped by Julie's classroom. She got tears in her eyes as she bent down to give Teddy a treat and rhythmically stroke his back. She told him thanks for visiting her cousin. Then she looked up at me and explained her cousin had passed away the night before, only a few days after Teddy had been there.

I was stunned and gave her my condolences. I was also amazed that Teddy had somehow known to stop into that room. He was happy to see his "treat room friend," but had appeared as if there was another purpose to his visit. Evidently there was!

Once again, Teddy knew something we did not. His calm presence was exactly what was needed that day as he allowed a woman one last gentle touch to the head of a dog, before she left this world.

CHAPTER 4

Teddy and Kindergarten Separation Anxiety

Many kindergarteners come to school on their first days anxious about starting school. Many parents also do the same! Teddy has helped countless students, especially kindergarteners weave their way through this milestone. Kaylee, however, had one of the strongest, longest lasting difficulty separating. This helped her form a strong bond with Teddy, one I can say may be unparalleled with any other student in his 12.5 years.

It was the beginning of the school year in 2011 and Kaylee did not want to leave her mom's side on that first day. She clung to her desperately. Since she lived with her mom and grandparents at the time, her grandfather, lovingly called "Papa," decided maybe it would be better if he brought her instead. Kaylee would cry and cling to her papa as well. This went on day after day.

Finding Kaylee in this state, Teddy would offer his gentleness. She at first reluctantly responded. I would ask her if she would like to walk to class with Teddy and I or on her own. She of course would say with Teddy. Then I would ask her if she wanted me to hold his leash or if she wanted to hold it. She started out wanting me to hold it, but would take hold part way to her classroom. Slowly, she would make her way down the hall with Teddy's leash in her tiny fingers. She would slowly turn and offer a solemn goodbye to Papa, but she at least went without grasping and clinging. She would turn back and give a tiny little smile to Teddy and softly talk to him on their way to the classroom. She would tell him how she would miss her papa, but that Teddy helped her miss him less. Teddy seemed to understand as he trotted happily with her to her classroom.

Through Kindergarten, Kaylee developed a special bond with Teddy. She would come see him at lunch recess and caress his soft ears. She would tell him how she had made it through the morning and that there was just a little bit of time left to go before she could go home. She told Teddy coming to school and seeing him made it easier for her to leave home.

Kaylee loved Teddy and continued to have their "talks" throughout the years as various things would happen at school – a argument with a friend or how to handle someone picking on her or someone else. Once extremely bashful, she grew strong and assertive with Teddy's help. In second grade, she even came to tell us both how she stood up for a classmate who was getting bullied! Her parents and grandparents sang his praises for the way he helped Kaylee grow, all the way from day one.

Four years later, when Kaylee learned of his retirement, she wrote this heart-warming story about Teddy:

Teddy

When I was in kindergarten I cried because I was scared and then this dog came along and helped me. His name was Teddy. He came every day and helped me. I don't like to say this but he is retiring. I wish he would not. All I wanted was him to be here with me in fourth grade. Maybe someday I will see him again.

Her mother still says to this day, "I don't think Kaylee would have made it through Kindergarten without you and Teddy!"

Her grandmother, a former colleague of mine, told me, "It was Teddy's presence and calm, safe demeanor that brought Kaylee out of her separation anxiety. He helped her gain feelings of security and I will personally always appreciate and love Teddy!"

Teddy's calm way helped Kaylee realize she would be okay. He became that friend that's always there to listen over the years for her. He watched her grow and help someone else with her assertiveness skills. When Kaylee told me how sad she was that he was retiring, I quoted Dr. Seuss and said, "Don't cry because it's over, Kaylee. Smile because it happened." We smiled together.

CHAPTER 5

Chad is Really Mad

We had a student I'll call Chad one particular school year with significant behavior issues. Our Behavior Disorder (BD) teacher had tried and tried this particular day to calm him down. He was screaming, throwing things, tipping tables over, even attempting to run out of the building. His behaviors came in waves. He'd settle down only to rise again to an uncontrollable level. She had worked with him literally for hours. Finally, she prepared to contact the principal. She knew in situations such as this, it was time to contact Chad's mother, describe his behavior, and suggest she take him home for the day, since he was out of instructional control.

As the teacher prepared for this phone call, I happened to pass by with Teddy and stopped to talk to someone in a nearby classroom. The boy was in a wave of only mild agitation, mostly making noise at this point, but not flailing his body about; however, given his pattern that day, it seemed possible it could start again at any moment.

Teddy, who usually stays right by my side, seemed to sense something was wrong and slowly made his way to the room where Chad was with his head down to show submission (dog language for "I respect you and mean no harm"). I have never taken Teddy into a situation where a student was out of control to a point where Teddy could get hurt. Teddy usually seems to know he needs to keep his distance with a "stay" command. Noticing Teddy going toward the classroom, I went to the door and assessed the situation. It seemed safe for Teddy to go to the child, as long as the BD teacher agreed. We didn't want to "reward" his poor behavior, but it seemed as if Teddy knew something we didn't. So we let Teddy go to Chad.

Chad began to stroke Teddy's soft head and ears, then his back. As his strokes lengthened, he began to breathe easier. His facial contortions faded to a more relaxed, almost serene state. Teddy lay on the floor and rolled over on his back (another sign of submission for a dog) and let the boy continue to pet him. Chad began to grin, slowly at first. Then his smile grew. He began to talk ever so gently to Teddy, in a rather high pitched voice. Teddy continued his "magic," rolling from one side to the other, back and forth. The BD teacher, para, and I watched in awe at the seeming miracle Teddy was performing right before our eyes! He was transforming Chad into a relaxed, at ease child!

After about 10 minutes, Chad looked up at his BD teacher and in a loving voice said, "I love Teddy! I can't pet him all day, though. I have some work I need to finish." The BD teacher and I exchanged glances of amazement as this child, who only 15 minutes earlier was out completely out of instructional control, decided on his own, get his work finished! Teddy had performed quite the transformation for Chad! Chad ended up not only staying the rest of the day, but finishing all of his work! The BD teacher called at the end of the day to see if Teddy could come up for a celebration for just a few minutes before Chad went home. It was quite a turn around.

Teddy seemed to know Chad needed him. Sensing his high tension level Teddy went to him, and simply let Chad pet him. It had appeared as if Chad would need to go home due to his behavior and lack of instructional control. We were unable to help Chad that day; however, with Teddy's help, Chad eventually calmed down enough to complete his work and stay at school for the entire day. Teddy helped us help Chad. Teddy had known just what to do and when to do it!

CHAPTER 6

Autism, Teddy, and a Fire Drill

One of our most profoundly Autistic children I have ever worked with, Jacob, entered Kindergarten with a diagnosis of Autism Spectrum Disorder. He had only recently been diagnosed, and parents were reaching out to us as a school to help them with their son's behavior. Loud noises bothered him. Bright lights bothered him. If Jacob got out of his routine, even just a little, he went into a full blown tantrum. Needless to say, we had our hands full. On the other side, Jacob had an amazing brain and could remember things after hearing them only once. He could read full books in kindergarten. He knew the most intricate details about dinosaurs, having read any and all books he could get his hands on. And he loved dogs! He was the most gentle spirit when it came to dogs. Needless to say, Teddy was a real hit with him!

When the principal informed our staff that we would be having a fire drill coming soon, we knew we would have to somehow prepare Jacob for this. It would be a change in routine, the alarm would be loud, and the lights from the alarms would be flashing. All of the things that set him off would be happening all at once! We couldn't keep him from it, since he needed to be prepared like all the other children.

I talked with the teacher about utilizing Teddy. I took Teddy to Jacob and explained to him we would be having a fire drill soon. His teacher described what a fire drill was, what it looked like, and what it sounded like. We also told Jacob that his job would be to get out of the building quickly with the rest of the students. We could see the anxiety rise in him. I asked him if he would help me with Teddy on that day. I told him how sensitive Teddy's ears were to the sound. Though Teddy had been a champ through dozens of fire drills, I asked Jacob if he could reassure Teddy that it would be okay, that it was only a drill, and that they needed to practice getting to safety quickly. He happily agreed!

So when the fire drill day arrived, I took Teddy to Jacob just moments before the alarm would sound. I reminded him of what he needed to tell Teddy during this drill. He was more than proud to help this dog he loved. I could see it in his eyes and his puffed up chest, even at age five!

The alarm sounded. Piercing, high pitched noises rang rhythmically through the hallway. The lights flashed. Jacob ever so calmly took Teddy's leash in his hand and began to stroke Teddy's head. As he stroked him, he calmly repeated to Teddy over and over, "It's okay, Teddy. It's only practice. I know it's loud. It's loud for me too, but we have to get outside quickly and safely. Then it will be all over. You can do this. It's okay, Teddy." He continued to repeat this over and over as Teddy heeled between me and Jacob. All the while he was talking to Teddy, he was actually telling himself those things as well! He was using a strategy called positive self- talk to get him through a difficult situation! I glanced at the teacher, who was wide-eyed, jaw in a half grin, half drop, watching this take place.

Jacob made it all the way out the door and to the safety of the parking lot where the school met. He made it! He did it! I thanked him over and over for "helping Teddy" get through this fire drill. We did this for the first tornado drill as well as the first intruder drill that year for Jacob. He came to realize himself, through "helping Teddy," that even though it was loud and out of his routine, it would soon be over, and most importantly, he could do it!

Therapy dogs are an amazing benefit to children with Autism and can be utilized in so many ways. When he was telling Teddy it would be okay even though it was loud, he was also telling himself the same thing. Teddy helped Jacob by letting Jacob believe he was helping Teddy!

CHAPTER 7

Teddy and a Special Anniversary

It was about a week before the end of the school year in 2015, the year Teddy retired. He and I were walking out of the office before school started, past three adults, two of whom were involved in a conversation. One was a young mom of a kindergarten student, the other was another kindergartener's grandmother. They were waiting to go on a field trip that morning with the children.

Teddy usually stayed right by my side as we moved through the building. This morning, he changed his path and veered over toward the older woman. She had her back turned to him and was startled as he nudged her elbow with his nose to get her attention, in typical Teddy-fashion. She gave out a little gasp and looked down to see what was "wet" at her elbow! I'll never forget the changes of emotion which crossed that woman's face as she reached out to pet Teddy.

At first she giggled at her own reaction to his nose at her elbow. Then as she began stroking his soft head, she realized he was our school therapy dog and her gaze changed to amazement and a bit of awe as she held her other hand over her heart.

"Oh, Teddy! You just made my day," she said ever so softly and looked up at me and grinned.

Her eyes had a far-away look in them as she asked me in wonder,

"Do they know? I think dogs know. Does *he* know?"

I was confused as to what she was asking, and wondered what it was she thought he knew. I imagined it was some sort of emotional turmoil she may have been facing inside, but perhaps didn't wish to share with everyone present in the office at that moment.

So I simply said, "Teddy knows," with a reassuring look.

"Oh, I think he must!" She said with an imploring look that went from me back to Teddy.

She stroked his head several more times and bent and put her face to his face. She paused and looked at me, still with her hand over her heart.

"Today is the anniversary of my husband's death," she said ever so slowly. "I didn't think it was affecting me, but it must be. He knew."

My eyes filled with tears and all I could get out was, "Bless your heart!"

"Bless *his* heart, she replied, still stroking him.

Right down to his final days of work, he still knew when someone needed him. This woman, who didn't think she was struggling inside on the anniversary of her husband's death, still gave Teddy enough of a scent that he knew she needed some comfort. She needed some of "Teddy's Loving Care," even if only for a brief moment.

CHAPTER 8

The "Cool Teens" and the Parade

It was a warm October evening in 2013 as we walked in Clinton's annual "Mardi Gras" parade. This is a rather long parade, extending basically from the north end of our river town to the south end, approximately three miles. People lined the streets as I drove our vehicle through the parade pulling along a trailer of first graders for our son's Boy Scout troop. I brought Teddy, knowing onlookers would enjoy seeing him. He had walked alongside the convertible I drove the year before in the high school's homecoming parade and was a real hit.

I didn't think at his age of 11, however, he should walk the entire distance, as it is indeed a rather long route. I had Teddy get in the vehicle, but as he was trained and accustomed to doing, he stayed on the floor. I commanded him to get up over and over, but could not get him to get on the seat! What a good dog! But I had to have him up there so people could see him from the window. So I lifted him into the seat. But he jumped down onto the floor. I lifted him up again and commanded him to stay.

He looked at me humbly, and lay down on the seat. He was on the seat, yes, but lying down! Still no one could see him! I decided to have another adult drive our vehicle and I got out and walked with Teddy. I thought he could walk part of the parade and if he got tired, I could then have him get in the vehicle and rest. I should have known better than to think this spry, happy Golden Retriever, even at age 11, would want to rest when there were people there to see!

Teddy worked the crowd. With his tail wagging, he trotted along happily, first right by my side on the leash. As we made our way through the parade route, there were children shouting,

"Teddy! Mom, look! It's Teddy! He's in the parade!"

I had to extend the leash to its full length so he could greet all of his "peeps!" He greeted young and old alike. They extended their hands and we would move toward them so they could get in a quick pet. Teddy was certainly a happy dog! He was in his element … people everywhere! I imagined him thinking to himself how nice it was for all of these people to come out and see *him!*

We neared the end of the route and Teddy was still happily trotting along when three teenagers saw him. They were standing there in their oversized, saggy denims, baggy sweatshirts, and baseball caps pulled down, masking their eyes. They had their hands shoved into their pockets, and their body language suggested how seemingly bored they were with this "childish" parade. I did not recognize them as former Whittier students, but they recognized Teddy.

Before they could stop themselves, two of them shouted excitedly in unison, just like they did when they were in elementary school, "Teddy!"

Then they caught themselves and realized their façade of being bored with this parade was now shot.

One of the boys caught my grin, shot his hands quickly back into his pockets, and elbowed the other, saying, "It's Teddy," trying to sound as bored as he wished to appear.

Teddy didn't buy into all of their newfound teenage "coolness." He trotted right over to those three boys, as if not one day had gone by since he had seen them last. Those three teenage boys quickly lost themselves as they bent over and vigorously pet Teddy's head and patted his back. They were driven right back to the zeal they had for this animal when they were 8 years old. Teddy lingered a moment longer than he did with the rest of his "fan club" before trit-trotting on to the next group of outstretched hands. The three boys watched him move on with big grins on their faces and I overheard them talking about what a "cool" dog Teddy was and how they remembered him from their elementary days.

Leave it to a dog like Teddy to bring back happy memories of childhood; to simpler times when these boys could be spontaneous with their excitement. For a moment they were taken back to those days and forgot the social pressures they felt to be the "cool teenagers" they had now become.

That's quite an impact, for an animal to be able to continue to draw out affection from others. Teddy did it with ease as he kept their "secret" that they were really still those little boys inside all along.

CHAPTER 9

School is Teddy's Second Home

We live in Clinton, Iowa, which is about 90 miles south of my hometown, Platteville, Wisconsin. One Saturday in 2009, I took my kids back to visit my parents for the weekend. My husband, Wes, stayed home. Being a police officer, he was working the night shift from 6:00 pm to 6:00 am all weekend. My Mom doesn't let animals into her house, so we left Teddy at home with Wes.

Wes came home on a break about 9:00 pm Saturday night. Teddy seemed anxious to get outside, so Wes let him out. Wes got interrupted during his break, as frequently happens in police work, and had to leave quickly. He called to Teddy to come inside, but Teddy wouldn't. This was rather unusual, because Teddy usually does what he is told. He just simply lay down in the grass and refused to budge. My husband had to get to this call and had no time to waste, so he left with his sirens blaring, thinking he would be able to get back soon and let Teddy back in.

As it often goes on a Saturday night on duty, Wes got busy going call to call and never made it back until about 3:00 am to let Teddy inside. When he pulled into our driveway, he didn't see Teddy anywhere! He shouted and whistled, thinking perhaps he was in the back, but Teddy did not come. He went inside and opened the back door, shouting and whistling for Teddy to come, but still no Teddy.

We have an underground fence, and Teddy usually did not leave the yard because of it, so this was confusing to say the least. Beginning to get worried, he walked around outside our house as well as the neighbors' houses, calling to Teddy. Nothing. Thinking himself in quite a bit of trouble for losing not only our family pet, but also the school therapy dog, he got in his squad car and turned the spotlight on, driving all around our neighborhood, window down, calling for Teddy. Teddy was nowhere to be seen. He was concerned – not only would his wife and kids be upset, but so would 400 elementary school children! "Worry" didn't describe the feeling in the pit of his stomach at that moment!

When he arrived home at 6:15 am, he again searched the neighborhood, hoping maybe the dawning sun would provide more opportunity to find a lost dog. Still nothing. He came back inside about 7:00 am and lay down on the couch. With a sinking feeling, he called the Law Center and reported Teddy missing.

At about 7:30 am, just as Wes was beginning to drift off into a restless sleep, our telephone rang and woke him. On the other end, someone asked him if he had a dog named Teddy. Excitedly he told them he did! They said they found him as they were on a walk … past Whittier Elementary School! He was lying at the front doors!

Poor Teddy missed his Mom (me!) and made his way, about two miles from home, up to Whittier where we worked, looking for me! He was patiently waiting, evidently, for Monday morning and his "mom" to come get him! I guess he thought I would be back eventually so he decided to lie down and wait. Thank goodness someone was on a Sunday morning walk and found him!

CHAPTER 10

The Visitation

It was early spring, a time of new life, when we received sad news that one of our first grader's dad had died. He had been terminally ill with cancer, and we knew it was coming, but nothing prepares anyone enough when it affects such a young child. Just seven years old and she had lost her daddy. Her mother called and told me of the sad news. She asked if I would speak with her daughter. Teddy and I talked with Sara a couple of times before the funeral. She would brush Teddy and talk about memories of her daddy.

When the visitation day arrived, I decided I needed to attend. After school, Teddy and I made our way to the funeral home. I'm learning now that area funeral homes are beginning to utilize therapy dogs, but at this time, it was not common to see a person enter a funeral home with a dog. Even though he had his halter on, showing he was an assistance dog, I still felt somewhat out of place with him.

The death of a young person draws a large crowd at funeral homes, and this visitation was no different. I had a few quizzical looks as I approached the door, but the funeral home's door man didn't bat an eye as we walked to him. I explained who I was as well as Teddy, and he just nodded and motioned me past him with his outstretched hand.

Sara was in back, but news of Teddy's arrival must have spread quickly, because she was out front within minutes. It was so touching as I watched her kneel in front of Teddy and look directly into his eyes as she gently stroked the top of his head. Teddy seemed to just know she needed him, because he did not budge. A counselor gets accustomed to strong emotion, but witnessing this brought tears to my eyes. She looked up at me and asked if I could bring Teddy to meet her mom. I handed Sara the leash. When I lifted my eyes to find her mom near the casket, I discovered her mom's gaze already on us. She had such a look of appreciation in her eyes as Teddy and Sara made their way to her mother. Sara's mom pet Teddy and thanked me for coming, and especially for bringing Teddy. She said Sara had remarked how much she adored Teddy.

Sara took me from the casket to show me the pictures of her father which they had on easels around the funeral home. As we passed people, they would ask if they could pet him. I of course said they could. I explained who Teddy was and what his job was. Teddy once again began to work the crowd, as he frequently did at school. Golden Retrievers always seem to have a smile on their faces, and Teddy had this smile, but with an ever-so humble appearance at the same time. He just wandered through the chairs of people and let them pet him one by one. He seemed to know just how long to stay before moving forward. I was amazed, since he had never been in a situation such as this before.

As it came time to go, Sara walked me to the door. I heard many say as they watched us leave what a nice idea it was to have him there, and what a great dog he was. I couldn't agree with them more! Sara squeezed Teddy around the neck and told him goodbye. She had a special bond with Teddy after that. She came to see us frequently in the weeks to follow, sometimes struggling with the loss, other times just to say hello to Teddy.

Though Teddy had never been in funeral home type of situation before, he still sensed what he needed to do and did it humbly with ease and grace. Most importantly, he was there for Sara. Beyond that, he also gave comfort to the many people who were paying their last respects to the family of such a young person leaving this world.

CHAPTER 11

Teddy Isn't Just for Students

Teddy's main job was to be there for the students; however, I saw time and time again that he was also there for the adults. I was involved in several parent meetings as the school counselor. Many times parents were hearing difficult pieces of information, maybe for the first time, from us, either in the way of academics or behavior of their children. Even in the best of these meetings, when everyone is in agreement, there is still some tension in the air.

Teddy came with me everywhere I went, so he was in these meetings with us. It was amazing to me, even after working with him for over 12 years, how he would instinctively go to whoever seemed to be having difficulty, no matter how subtle. I'm sure to the outsider, it appeared as if he was just randomly roaming to gain attention from people, but I knew this wasn't the case.

He was trained to go under the table or lie on the floor where I would tell him to go. I witnessed hundreds of times, literally, where he would be resting quietly. Tensions might rise - maybe it was in the tone of a voice or the uneasy shifting of a person in a chair, but Teddy would get up and go to that individual.

There were a couple of teachers I worked with whose only outward signal that they were upset was a botchy red discoloration which would begin at the base of their neck and move upward toward their jaw. Their voices would remain calm and they wouldn't even shift in their chair. Other than that, there would be no outward indication that their blood pressure was on the rise! Time and time again, Teddy would get up and go straight to that person, nudging their elbow with his nose, as he did. I would watch them begin to stroke his head and back, and watch the redness go away.

Many would talk to me afterward and remark about how appreciative they were that Teddy came to them at just the right moment. I knew this was more than "luck." I knew Teddy had a real sense for when individuals were struggling on the inside. I would watch people's faces relax, their breaths grow longer and more rhythmic, and their hands stop fidgeting as he worked his "magic" with them.

Even a parent came to me once after a rather intense special education meeting. He told me how he was feeling upset during the meeting, but Teddy just instinctively got up and came to him exactly when he needed it.

They say when we humans are upset, anxious, nervous, etc. we give off a particular scent that dogs can recognize, and some react to, with their highly developed sense of smell. This is how Teddy must have known people needed him in these meetings. Teddy was there for all of us, not just the students!

CHAPTER 12

Teddy's Search for Bob

We live in a very friendly neighborhood in the Midwest. Our next door neighbors are a very sweet, elderly couple, Bob and Jackie. They always liked Teddy and were amazed at the fact that he worked at a school. In their younger years, they would watch Teddy for us if we were going to be gone overnight. Teddy enjoyed visiting with them. At first, they wondered why he would stay in our yard and just look at them with his big brown eyes and wag his tail but not come over. I explained to them that we had an underground fence system which beeped to remind him to stay in our yard if he got too close to our property line. He rarely went over it, as he would get a subtle shock that he didn't like very much!

Once, when Teddy was young, there were Mallard ducks that had nested in Bob and Jackie's front bushes. One duck was wandering around their front lawn, and it was just too much for Teddy to resist! He chased after that Mallard duck as it flew just a few feet off the ground, all the way down the street! It felt as if I was in slow motion shouting after him, "Noooooo! Teddddddddyyyyyyyyy!!" as he ran all the way down the block. Bob and Jackie laughed and laughed at this, while my heart was in a state of panic!

Teddy, Bob, and Jackie became good friends. They would come to the edge of the property to say hello to Teddy, pet him and enjoy visiting. I could always tell when Teddy's fence collar would run out of battery because he would wander over and visit Bob and Jackie in their back screened in porch. They adored Teddy, especially Bob. He was outside quite a bit and got around very well.

As happens sometimes with age, Bob grew ill. He battled infection after infection for about a year. During the winter of 2015, I noticed tracks in the snow from our house. They went into Bob and Jackie's yard, past the screened in porch, around their house, and back to the front yard. I even caught him doing this once, and scolded him. At first I thought he was being a bit of a devil and changed the shock collar battery so he would stay in our yard. Then I began to notice these tracks continued on and off. They would be more prevalent when Bob was ill in the hospital! Teddy was watching over Jackie for Bob! He was sensing something was wrong and risking a shock to leave our yard in order to check on Jackie. He needed to be sure everything was okay … maybe he was even looking for Bob!

The summer that Teddy retired, I hadn't noticed Teddy in Bob and Jackie's yard very often (although there was no snow to leave evidence behind!). One particular day, it was extremely hot – so hot, the weather man had cautioned pet owners to keep their pets inside. Teddy loves being outside, so I would let him out for a while, then bring him back in. My husband and children had gone on a camping trip and I stayed home. I had come and gone a lot that day running errands, each time letting Teddy either outside or back in, since I was solely responsible for Teddy while my family was out of town.

On the return of one of my errands, Bob's daughter came out and told me she had seen Teddy outside, thought maybe we were all gone on vacation, and beckoned Teddy to come into her mother's house and "visit," so he wouldn't get overheated. She said he had kept them company for a while and talked of how much they enjoyed him. It was then that she told me Bob was growing weaker in the hospital and struggling physically.

One evening about a week later, as we left for the nearby drive in movie, I noticed several cars at Bob and Jackie's house. This being rather unusual, I commented to my husband, wondering if something had happened to Bob.

The next morning, I let Teddy outside to go potty and went back upstairs to shower. As I lifted the shades on the East side of our room, guess where I saw Teddy! He was sniffing around Bob and Jackie's back porch, ever so slowly doing his circle! I didn't scold him or tell him to come home, as I knew something was up. Later that day, Bob's daughter came over and told my husband that Bob had passed away the day before. Teddy must have sensed something was wrong and was checking up on them! We gathered a fresh fruit container and took Teddy to visit Jackie while we gave her our sympathy for the loss of her husband.

I think Teddy knew that something was wrong that evening as well as over the snowy winter months while Bob was ill. That may have been why he was leaving our yard to trot around their house. Even in retirement, he still has an amazing sense of knowing when and where he is needed! This dog knows his purpose!

CHAPTER 13

The Senior and Teddy's Legacy

In 2015, our PE teacher had an outdoor event called "Field Day." This is an organized event when all students get to go outside by grade level and enjoy various physical activities. We had inflatable bounce houses, running races, ring tosses, etc. set up outside. Staff members worked at various stations as the students, arranged in small groups, made their way from one activity to the next every 15 minutes or so. Teddy and I were at the water and frozen fruit-pop station.

High school students volunteered to come to Whittier to help with this day. One particular student approached the area Teddy and I were working and began to pet him, somewhat mindlessly at first. Suddenly, her face changed as she realized who she was petting.

"Is this still Teddy?" she asked in amazement.

"Yes it is," I replied with a grin as I watched this young woman realize she was being reunited with an old friend. "He's retiring in just a few days when this school year is over," I added.

Her eyes filled with tears and she put her hand over her mouth. "Oh my goodness!" she gasped. "I can't believe this is still him! I remember him from kindergarten here! Is this *really* still Teddy?! I can't believe we're both going to be done at the same time!"

She went on to talk about how much she loved seeing him when she was in elementary school.

"He was just so lovable and playful! Awww … Teddy …" and her words faded off as she bent over and stroked his soft face as tears of childhood memories streamed down hers.

Teddy left quite a legacy behind him. As our district's longest working therapy dog of 12.5 years, he saw many students, like this young lady, through their elementary years and into adulthood. He was there for them, whether it be just for a quick pet as he made his way down the hall with me, for one-on-one time as students worked through problems, or for a fun-filled game of "fetch" on the playground during recess. Teddy's Golden smile and wagging tail was there through it all. He leaves a legacy of joyous memories, forever in the hearts of all who knew him.

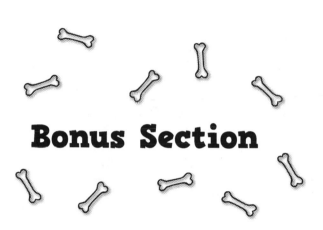

Bonus Section

CHAPTER 14

A Fun Reading Story From Teddy

In 2004, our school's Learning Resource Center Coordinator wanted to promote reading for students in recognition of Read Across America Week and Dr. Seuss' 100th Birthday. She asked Whittier faculty members to submit a story of their favorite reading memory. The following story is what I submitted for Teddy.

No bones about it … I remember my favorite reading memory like it was just a dog-day ago! That first reading memory has made me the dog I am today!

I was a mere pup at the time. I remember lying all snug and cozy in my mama's paws. While my brothers and sisters were busy chasing their tails, I was intently listening to the humans in the next room read a book about a dog named, "Clifford." They read different <u>Clifford</u> books each night. Clifford was such a gentle dog, who loved children. Clifford was a big red dog. I looked at my coat. My fur was sort of red! Maybe someday I could be a big, gentle, red dog, just like Clifford! I fell asleep each night dreaming I, too, had an "Emily Elizabeth," and a home with humans.

One morning, when I woke up, there was a lady with black hair talking about needing a dog for a place called "school." Her name was Karla. I wondered what this place called "school" was like. I wondered if there would be more <u>Clifford</u> books or an "Emily Elizabeth" there. It sounded like a fun place to be. I wanted more than anything to go with Karla! I sat as straight and tall as I could and wished with all my heart that she would pick me. She did! I was so excited!

The next day, Karla took me to a special place called "Whittier School." I looked all around … there wasn't just one "Emily Elizabeth!" There were hundreds of "Emily Elizabeths" there! Everywhere I looked! There was a Shawn Michael, a Brian Wesley, a Claire Marie! And I was bigger than they were! And I was a red dog!

My dream to be just like Clifford had really come true!

My love for books has grown since those first days of <u>Clifford</u>. I love listening to children read! My boys and girls at home have read <u>Lassie</u> to me, <u>Dog at the Door,</u> <u>McGrowl</u> and a series called, <u>The Puppy Place</u> too. At Whittier, Kindergarteners come in and read to me and Karla! The students there carry books with them everywhere – they have them in their desks and their book bags too! Each month they take book orders home to their parents. Twice each year, they have a big Book Fair put on by the PTA (they're the group that helped me get to this wonderful place!). The students get to have a fun trading day each year called, "book exchange," that Sherry in the Family Resource Center organizes (she's the other nice lady who takes care of me sometimes). They even have a whole entire room called an L.R.C. (Learning Resource Center), that's filled with books of all kinds! In the LRC, students get to take books home with them if they want (and I get yummy dog treats there sometimes too – added bonus!).

The children at Whittier are so lucky to be learning and reading so much. I am also lucky to be the dog to whom they read!

CHAPTER 15

Atta Boy Teddy

Elementary school children are very open with their affection, especially toward animals such as Teddy. Teachers would have students practice letter writing in various grade levels by writing to staff members. Teddy received some of these letters. Other students randomly wrote love notes to Teddy on their own, pouring out their affection for him!

I have kept a file over the years from students who've written their love notes to Teddy. I call the folder, "Atta Boy." I share some of these with you to show you the love they had for this dog.

You'll notice many refer to Teddy's ties … Teddy had several ties which he wore at school each day. "He" tried to match whatever I was wearing. People really enjoyed seeing him in his ties!

Dear Teddy, I like the way you are a good dog. You are a real good listener. You are good in guidance and you are a good friend
~ Grade 1

Dear Teddy,
Thank you for being our therapy dog at Whittier School! You make me feel happy when I feel sad. You can help me feel better when I am sad by helping me.
~ Grade 1

Dear Teddy:
We appreciate that you are our therapy dog. Teddy, you are:
Cool, awesome, amazing, adorable, active, soft, nice, and ...
AWESOME!!!
~ Grade 2

Teddy, You are the best! I love you Teddy!
~ Grade 1

Nice – Cool – Kind
Teddy is very nice.
Teddy is soft.

Teddy is awesome.
~ *Grade 2*

Ted – I Love Teddy – Dear Teddy,
You are a cool dog.
Teddy be happy.
Teddy is Awesome.
~ *Grade 2*

You're Amazing Teddy!
You're the best therapy dog.
You're the softest dog.
~ *Grade 2*

I like Teddy because he's soft. He's helpful. He's
kind. He's playful.
~ *Grade 2*

Happy Teddy,
Teddy is a kind dog.
He is an adorable doggie.
Teddy is a superstar
~ *Grade 2*

I like Teddy's handsome ties.
He is so soft and I appreciate him.
He is awesome and cool.
~ Grade 2

Teddy is the best!
Teddy is the best dog ever. Heis adorable, kind,
nice, short, playful, and active.
I love Teddy's ties. Some are so cool.
I love you Teddy!
~ Grade 2

Dear Teddy,
Thank you for always being there when I'm sad
and mad.
I love you!
~ Grade 2

Teddy,
You are nice Teddy.
You are a good dog.
You are a nice dog.
~ Grade 2

Teddy,
You're the best therapy dog in the world!
You're the best Golden Retriever!
~ Grade 2

Thank you Teddy
I Love you Teddy
You're the best dog ever!
~ Grade 1

Dear Teddy,
You are nice to us and you don't beg for food.
PS We love you
PS You are cute.
Thank you for being nice
~ Grade 1

I love Teddy!
Teddy you are my friend.
You are cute.
~ Grade 1

Teddy always lets us pet him
~ Grade 1

Dear Teddy,
You always cheer me up when I get left out and
mad. I will miss you when I move Friday.
~ *Grade 1*

Have a good summer. Go swimming.
I will miss you Teddy and Mrs. Unke
You are always there when we are sad and mad.
~ *Grade 1*

I love you Teddy!
You are the best dog in the world.
Thank you for making me laugh Teddy!
~ *Grade 1*

Teddy is always there when I'm sad.
He always lets us pet him.
He lets us read to him.
He's a good furry friend.
He does cool tricks.
Teddy wears nice ties.
He loves us.
He cheers us up.
He is the best dog I have ever seen!
~ *Grade 2*

Teddy,
You deserve an award for cheering me up when
I am sad.
~ *Grade 4*

Teddy, thanks for being there when I'm sad.
You are awesome!
~ *Grade 1*

Dear Teddy
You are a very good dog. You always help people
when they are sad. You're always our friend!
~ *Grade 1*

Teddy thank you for helping us feel better when
we are hurt.
~ *Grade 1*

Dear Teddy,
I love you Teddy. You are the cutest dog I have
ever seen.
~ *Grade 2*

CHAPTER 16

Goodbye and Enjoy Retirement Teddy

In 2015, Teddy retired after 12.5 years of devotion to Whittier Elementary School students, parents, and staff. He was the longest working therapy dog in the Clinton Community School District. I will be forever indebted to the parents on the Whittier PTA during the 2002-2003 school year who approved the money for the Teddy's training. He has been an amazing dog! I am grateful for this journey with him!

Below are just some of the messages contained in the notes and cards students made for him as they learned of his retirement (I have corrected spelling errors in some for ease of reading).

Happy Retirement Teddy!
Thank you for giving us TLC and we gave you TLC!!!!!!
~ *Grade 2*

I
Will
Not
Forget
You
Teddy
~ *Signed by each member of one 3rd grade classroom*

*If you've ever spent any length of time with an elementary student, you'll realize they call every female teacher "miss" (plus her last name), whether or not she is a Miss or a Mrs. Yet, they see our ID badges written beginning with "Mrs." Keeping that in mind, this one gives me a particular chuckle!

To Teddy:
I will Mrs. you.
~ *Grade 3*

To: Teddy Bear
I will be missing you Teddy. I hope I will see you again. I know you helped me in kindergarten. Thank you for helping me. Can you please stay, Teddy? I don't want you to retire. You are my

best friend. School is almost done. Can you please stay with me? I will miss you!
~ *Grade 3*

All About Teddy
Teddy is a Golden Retriever. He is yellowish brownish. He is Whittier's therapy dog. He is very very nice. He belongs to the Unkes. Sometimes he comes to our class for Guidance. Everyone loves Teddy! But something very sad is going to happen. Teddy is retiring. But one thing is for sure. We will always love Teddy.
~ Grade 3

The adults loved him too … He got many gifts (mostly dog bones!) and cards at a retirement party for him and other honored staff members who had also given years of service to our students.

Dearest Teddy,
Woof woof woof woof woof woof, woof woof woof!! TRANSLATED TO:
I will miss seeing you every day here at school …
~ *Staff Member*

Unke Family and Teddy,

Thank you so much for letting me get to love and know your beautiful Teddy.

Mr. Teddy, Enjoy your Golden years. Take it easy.

~ Staff Member

I even received a petition not to have him retire, from a third grade classroom!

We will miss Teddy! We don't want Teddy to retire. We want to see him next year!

~ Grade 3 (names of one entire classroom of students!)

To Teddy Unke,

Teddy is the best dog ever. I wish he was not retiring. He loved Whittier. But at least he can come and visit. If he knew, he'd be sad and maybe mad. If he were to stay, he would be staying at least until I'm in 6th grade. I Love Teddy and I like to see him every day, including being at school. But every day when I get back home I'm going to greet him. And I know he'll greet us. TEDDY

~ Grade 3

Teddy Teddy I Love You!
I love you.
I will miss you so much.
You were a good therapy dog.
I will miss you.
You were great.
I love you.

Roses are red
Violets are blue.
I LOVE you!

I Love you so much!
~ Grade 2

Teddy Teddy, have a great life. We'll all miss you. We've had a great time together through Kindergarten, 1st, 2nd, but not 3rd, 4th, or 5th because you are retiring now. I'll miss you and everybody else will too. Goodbye.
Teddy you are awesome
~ Grade 2

Teddy I'm going to miss you. We appreciate you very much. Your ties are super cute. You have been very fun playing with. You have helped me be comfortable in Kindergarten when I was new.

~ Grade 5

To Teddy! We appreciate Teddy!
Mrs. Unke, Teddy is so cute, kind, and soft. He is so playful and active too. We'll all miss Teddy. Teddy is so nice and cute too. That's why we'll miss Teddy so much, Mrs. Unke.
Bye Teddy. We'll miss you.

~ Grade 5

(I don't know why this line is here – I can't get rid of it! Please remove for printing of book)

Get that bacon tie!
Teddy is awesome.
You are a good therapy dog.
You are very playful.
I will miss you Teddy bear!
Bacon tie!

~ Grade 2

A Good Therapy Dog!
Have a good retirement Teddy!

Dear Mrs. Unke,
I think Teddy is so cute, kind, with handsome
ties and I am surprised that he can run that fast
when he is playing with the kids.
I think he has been so good for the three years
I have been here at Whittier School.
~ *Grade 2*

Dear Teddy,
Happy Retirement.
I hope you will miss us.
~ *Grade 2*

Dear Teddy and Mrs. Unke:
I do not think any dog will replace Teddy ever.
Teddy is the best therapy dog there will ever be!
TEDDY!
~ *Grade 2*

Teddy,
I will miss you very much Teddy.
PS
Can you come back and visit us, Teddy?
~ Grade 2

I love you Teddy!
I am going to miss you <u>SO</u> much.
I hope you come to visit.
I love you Teddy
~ Grade 2

Teddy,
I will miss you.
I will love you.
You are in our hearts.
We will always love you!
~ Grade 3 classroom

T eddy Bear
E xcellent
D elightful
D etermined
Y oung at heart

Teddy
This is how I describe Teddy.
He is my Teddy Bear
He is excellent.
He is delightful.
He is so determined.

Most of all he is young at heart.
We all will always love you Teddy!
~ Grade 3

"Teedy" (Teddy!)
T is for Together
E is for 'Encredible' (incredible!)
E is for Excellent
D is for Dick Chaney
Y is for you're awesome!

We will miss you 'Teedy'!
We will never forget you 'Teedy'!
~ Grade 3 classroom

Dear Teddy,
You are very calm and sweet and very very well trained. I have enjoyed 6 years with you.

Dear Mrs. Unke,
You are very nice and helpful. Thank you for helping me through my parents' divorce. You are wonderful at helping people and handling Teddy.
~ Grade 5

Karla Unke

To Teddy
Teddy Teddy
We Love you
We Love you
We will never forget you
Even when you are gone
Teddy we will miss you.
We love you.
We did not forget you.
We love you Teddy
xoxox
~ Grade 1

You made me cry because you are leaving. I hope you can come back to school and stay.
Teddy always lets me pet him and he helps me if I get hurt. You are helpful. He cheers me up. He loves me and he loves dog treats. He helps us feel happy if we are sad.
Teddy's loving care. This makes me cry because I feel sad.
~ Grade 1

Dear Teddy,
I know I won't see you again but here is something you need to know. You made me cry because you are leaving.
~ *Grade 1*

We love you Teddy even when you're not here.
~ *Grade 1*

Roses are red
Violets are blue
You're the best dog
We love you.
~ *Grade 1*

Teddy,
If you would stay I would give you "TLC" (Teddy's Loving Care).
We love you!
Have fun Teddy!
~ *Grade 1*

Love Teddy,
You are the best and I will miss you because I love you Teddy.

I hope I see you.
~ *Grade 1*

You are the best dog ever. I will miss you.
You are the best dog. I will miss you Teddy.
Goodbye. You are a sweet dog. Teddy cheers
you up if you get left out.
~ *Grade 3*

I love our teddy bear
Teddy you are sweet. You make me happy. I
like you Teddy bear. You're always there when
I'm sad.
~ *Grade 1*

Dear Teddy,
We love you Teddy. We are your tender care.
Teddy cheers us up when we get lonely.
We love you Teddy.
We love you Teddy.
We love you Teddy.
We love you Teddy!
We love you Teddy!
We love you Teddy!

We love you Teddy!
Yes, we love you Teddy!!
~ *Grade 1*

Teddy,
Teddy you are tender loving care.
Teddy you are loved.
~ *Grade 1*

Teddy was an awesome therapy dog, but a dog's gotta do what a dog's gotta do. Luckily I can still see him. See ya!! Bye Teddy!
~ *Grade 2*

I love you so much Teddy
You are the best Teddy
I will miss you.
I hope you visit us sometime.
I will miss you so much.
You were the best therapy dog.
I love you so much.

Roses are red Violets are blue
Honey is sweet
I will miss you.
~ *Grade 2*

Happy retirement day!
Teddy is there when I'm sad and feeling left out.
Teddy is a great dog and he is the best because he is a good boy. Can Teddy come sometimes?
~ Grade 2

Dear Teddy,
Thank you for working at our school so long.
I like your ties.
Have a good retirement.
You are my friend.
~ Grade 2

Dear Teddy,
I love you. Thank you and you will always remain in my heart.
~ Grade 2

Teddy is an awesome dog.
Teddy when you leave I will miss you very much. Teddy I love you. Do you have to leave Teddy? Can you come visit us Teddy, please Teddy, please!
Bye! Come back and visit!
~ Grade 2

I'm going to miss you so much. I love you Teddy.
It's so sad you're leaving. I love Teddy.
~ Grade 2

Dear Teddy,
I think you and your ties are cute and awesome.
I will miss you Teddy. I was just crying because
I missed you so bad. Have a good retirement.
You are so cute!
~ Grade 2

Happy retirement Teddy!
I like the way he's always there when I am sad.
We will miss you Teddy.
~ Grade 2

Dear Teddy:
You are always my best friend ever!
I hope you visit us!
Thank you Mrs. Unke!
~ Grade 2

Dear Teddy,
I hope you come visit. You're the best. You're a
good furry friend
~ Grade 3

Thank you Teddy for helping me.
I love you Teddy.
You are very nice Teddy.
I love you Teddy.
I will think about you Teddy.
~ Grade 2

Teddy I wish you could stay here. You help me
when I am here and sad. I love you Teddy. Have
fun at home next year. I will miss you.
~ Grade 1

CHAPTER 17

Things I've Learned from Teddy

🐾 Paws are for holding 🐾 Stay with your pack 🐾 Live life to the fullest 🐾 Wag your tail when you're happy 🐾 Good things come to those who wait ... patiently 🐾 People will always remember the way you made them feel 🐾 Be ready for a belly rub at a moment's notice 🐾 Comfort should never be denied 🐾 SOAR'ing is important (At Whittier we "SOAR" – We are Safe, Organized, Accountable, and Respectful) 🐾 Loving dogs is a sign of good character 🐾 Always give people a friendly freeting 🐾 A gentle nudge for more attention never hurt 🐾 Be loving every chance you get 🐾 A friendly game of "tug o' war" can be team building 🐾 Leave room in your schedule for a good nap 🐾 Always be ready for a spontaneous hug 🐾 Adore the hand of the one who feeds you 🐾 Treat yourself daily 🐾 Tennis ball ...

only the BEST – TOY – EVER! ❧ You're never too old to learn new tricks ❧ Make time to play ❧ Every kid deserves a dog ❧ Whittier rocks! ❧ Everyone needs a Teddy Bear to love every now and then ❧ Take time to smell for treats ❧ Neckties can be distinguishing ❧ Get outside a little bit every day ❧ The first day of school is always exciting ❧ Domestic life is alright ❧ Reading is a treat ❧ You're never too big to sit on someone's lap ❧ There's Always Time to "PAWS" for a Little TLC (Teddy's Loving Care)!

If you enjoyed this book, you may also enjoy Karla (Wunderlin) Unke's first book about Teddy! <u>Teddy's Loving Care (TLC)</u> <u>- The Work of a School Therapy Dog</u> is a children's book about the training, personality, and job of a school therapy dog. This book is filled with actual full color photographs of Teddy himself, in his role as a Certified Professional Therapy Dog.
Available at Authorhouse.com.

Printed in the United States
By Bookmasters